Keep More of Your Money

Keep More of Your Money

Seven Ways to Keep More of What You Make

www.keepmoremoneybook.com

Michael Andrews

Cover design by Michael Andrews using Kindle Direct
Publishing Cover Creator
First Edit by Kristin Roth (Roth Editorial Services:
www.rotheditorial.com)
Final Edit by Michael Andrews

Contents

Introduction

Numerous money books focus on making more money. This book may help you do that, but here, we will focus on seven principles that will help you keep more of what you make. You will also learn how to get more out of your precious time, energy, and effort. The news headlines today are littered with stories of people who made a lot of money but wound up broke. **Making money means nothing unless you know how to keep it.**

Believe it or not, everyone is successful: some are successful at having money, others are successful at never having money, and some are successful at being somewhere in between. The principles that we will discuss will help you have "whole life" success—because when you have whole-life success, better management of your finances will be a natural result. When your life is in order, your money works for you—not the other way around. The information in this book is now yours and will work for you as long as you choose to use it—you'll never have to buy anything else.

Who will benefit from this book? Everybody. Whether you are a single mother running a household or a CEO running a multi-million-dollar business, this book will help you. Even if your financial life is in order, the principles in this book will reinforce and sharpen what you already know. People and circumstances change constantly, but these principles do not. You will learn how to apply them to your changing life circumstances to get more consistent results.

Keep reading and you will learn how to have more money without having to convince anyone else to do or buy anything. You will learn how to shrewdly manage what you can control and how to react properly when the inevitable negatives of life come upon you. Our reactions are just as important as our actions. We can control both, and when we do that right, it will positively affect not just our money but our peace of mind, health, and relationships.

Now we must discuss what this book is not and what it will not do. First and foremost, it is not a get-rich-quick book. The principles taught here work over time, and the longer you use them, the better your results will be. Secondly, if you are deeply in debt, this book will not get you out of your circumstances overnight. It will, however, help you improve your situation over the long run. Lastly, this book is not a guarantee against all financial problems. We live in a world where bad things can and often do happen to even the most cautious people. In this book, you will learn to better manage what you control—not learn to control everything. No one can do that.

Before you continue reading, you should know that the principles in this book are easiest to apply in a free-market society. You should also know that I am not a financial or investment advisor, nor do I in any way recommend any investments to anyone. Any investments mentioned in what follows are for example purposes only. Similarly, any companies mentioned in what follows are used only to illustrate a point—I am not endorsing any of them. This book is for the purpose of information only. Please see the full disclaimer at the end of the book.

No one on planet earth can, or will, act in your best interest as well as you can. That is why applying the material here takes personal responsibility, self-motivation, self-discipline, and persistence. You must understand that you are never at a point where you will be finished applying this material. I know of many people who always had money and then lost it late in life with no remedy. Here you will learn some of the reasons this happens so that you do not fall into this situation yourself. The world out there is a jungle with pitfalls at every turn. Read on to learn not just how to survive but how to prosper in the years ahead!

1. Choose the Right Relationships

What is the first step in keeping more of your money? Quite simply, it is to choose the right relationships. The people in your life can be a gateway to happiness and prosperity, or they can let in suffering, hardship, and aggravation. Because there are both people who will help you and people who will harm you in the world, you must properly manage who is in your life and who is not. Every dollar that comes to you or leaves you comes from or goes to another person. Sometimes money comes or goes *because* of other people. That is why to keep more of your money you must first focus on the people in your life.

To have more money, peace of mind, and happiness, you must make gaining and maintaining good relationships with other people in your life your first priority. Your goal is to gain and maintain the good relationships in your life and get rid of the ones that are not good for you as quickly as possible. You must understand that having the right people in your life is the easiest way to have more money. Even large, lucrative companies get their wealth because of the right people. Think about a company like Apple. Founder Steve Jobs was a visionary who didn't just foresee what the technological world would be like but helped to actually shape it. But even the wisest and most capable people need other people to make their ideas a reality. Jobs found thousands of great people from all over the world to work together for him. These people are creative innovators and skillful at taking the products from the design stage all the way to store shelves. So many people love what they make that crowds will wait in long lines and pay top dollar to get Apple's newly released products. Quite simply, Apple is a tremendously lucrative company because it has wisely chosen which people are a part of it, which in turn has allowed it to maintain good relationships with its customer base. It is hard to find another company that generates such personal loyalty from its customers.

When your relationships—both personal and professional—are in order, your money will tend to follow suit most of the time. You can't control other people, but you do have a measure of control over what people are in your life. Chances are you chose your friends, your place of employment, and your spouse if you have one. Your financial life today is largely a result of those choices. That is why this chapter is the most important one in this entire book. All money problems are actually people problems. Once you understand that, you can then approach money issues where they really start, and identify people that are either helping you or hurting you financially and act accordingly. That said, however, sometimes the problem can be you. Though other people can do some pretty rotten things to you, it is important to remember that in order to keep more of your money, you must make sure that your reaction to people's bad behavior toward you is not worse than that behavior in the first place.

In addition to choosing your relationships, you must choose your actions in those relationships. True self-responsibility and self-interest are good things because they simultaneously benefit both you and those around you. The personal satisfaction of others in dealing with you is one of the biggest keys to having more money because it can attract even more good people into your life. Self-responsibility promotes good, mutually beneficial relationships in every area—from marriages to employee-employer relationships. Selfishness, on the other hand, is when people try to act in their own interest in a way that hurts other people. Yes, it is possible to have more money this way, but it is only temporary because selfishness always catches up with selfish people later on. There is a price to be paid for being that way. But when you act in your own best interest and are financially responsible, you are being good to others because you are freeing them of the responsibility of supporting you.

Do you want to gain all the good things in life? If you do, then you must give what you want to get. If you want to get a raise at work, make a point to act in your employer's best financial interest as much as possible. Want a great spouse? Be the best spouse you can be. Do you want to be respected by your coworkers? Respect your coworkers. Everything starts with you! The list could be endless, but you get the idea. You need to understand, though, that other people do not always automatically give back what you give. You must be very careful about what you give and who you give it to.

All that said, I am sure you can agree that your health is the greatest wealth that you can ever possess. What good is it to gain all the money in the world and then lose your health because of the stress you endured to get it? Right now, there is a millionaire dying somewhere who would give every penny he toiled for to have his health back and be able to spend more time with his family.

You are the most consistent factor in your life. No one on earth can respect you like you can. No one else can act in your own best interest as well as you can. Sometimes it is possible to not be "winning" financially (especially in the business world) because others are acting in their best interest and you are not acting in your best interest. The first step you want to take if you want to have any control over anything like relationships or money is to be your own best friend first and control yourself.

The first and most important relationship you have is the relationship with yourself. Give yourself every possible advantage you can financially. The following tips will help you do this and will enhance your relationships with others at the same time by making other people's relationships with you more pleasant and less burdensome.

- **Rest**. We feel pressured to work constantly today. Learn to say no to meaningless projects. Work is important, but without rest, you will wear yourself out physically and put your health in danger. There have been studies done that show that people's work time actually produces more per hour when people are rested. We are continually bombarded by social pressure and media of all kinds that say that we must have this and do that. This modern consumerism that is rampant today will have you running without rest if you let it. Learn to tune it out and only do what is good for you at a pace that is good for you, not for those trying to profit from you. The engine in your car won't last long if you hold the gas pedal to the floor all the time. You operate on the same principle. You can have millions of dollars and live in a mansion, but you will not enjoy it if you are exhausted all the time or—worse—in the hospital. When you fail to attain a goal but keep your health and peace of mind, you still win. Even the smartest people make poor decisions and have accidents that can be costly or fatal when they are exhausted.

- **Trade in your consumer mentality for an investment mentality**. Quite simply, good investments multiply your money, which in turn promotes rest and peace of mind later. Good investments make money for you while you sleep. If you have money to waste, you have money to invest. Let's pretend that someone gives two different people a handful of sunflower seeds each. The consumer-minded person insists on the instant gratification of eating the tasty seeds, and they are gone forever in a moment of passing pleasure. The investment-minded person delays his gratification, puts the seeds in good soil at the right time, and eventually gets sunflowers and many more sunflower seeds later. It works this way with money, too. As long as there are problems, there will also be future solutions to invest in and make more money.

- **Appreciate the simple things in life**. If you have your health, people in your life whom you love, food, and comfortable shelter, there are millions of people wishing they had what you are enjoying right now.

- **Deny yourself**. By denying yourself unnecessary spending, you are actually ridding yourself of the negative consequences that follow—namely, huge credit card bills, interest, and having to work harder unnecessarily. Denying yourself that expensive car that you really can't afford prevents you from being a slave to the bank. Why pay all that unnecessary interest to people whom you don't know and who don't care about you?

- **Give up spending money to save money**. When you buy something that you did not need because it was 40 percent off, you just spent 60 percent too much.

- **Keep in reserve a year's worth of expenses**. Your peace of mind will grow significantly when you have a year's worth of expenses in reserve because it will provide you with insulation between you and the negatives that can happen to you. Living paycheck to paycheck is a stressful joy killer that will rob your life of enjoyment and pleasure. It can also force you into bad relationships, like having to work for a sadistic employer in a dead-end job.

- **Break the association between people and things**. Here is an example: In America today, many people have a deep emotional dependence on food. This has happened because food has been eaten at holiday meals, weddings, and other festive events for centuries. Because of this, people often associate food with love, acceptance, and family togetherness. That is where the American term *comfort food* comes from. Yes, eating can be pleasurable, but there is no comfort in it. As a matter of fact, when you eat too much, it will make you very uncomfortable. The "comfort" that people experience from simply eating certain types of food is the reviving of memories of love and togetherness. Similarly, those who struggle with hoarding usually started engaging in their behavior after a loss of a relationship, whether through death, divorce, separation, or other means. They are trying to compensate for that personal loss with the accumulation of things. Then there are those who buy expensive clothes, cars, and houses, believing that this will win them the affirmation, approval, and acceptance of others. Though they may achieve their goal, it is because others approve of what they have, not of them personally. If you have to buy something to gain someone's approval, that person is not your friend. Remember—a love affair with food and all other inanimate objects is one sided. Food does not love you, and it never will. Neither will houses, boats, cars, or all the money in the world. Neither will people love you just for the fact that you have those things. Things are only there to serve you and others. They are there for our enjoyment and use but are very limited in their ability to make us happy compared to good relationships with others.

Here are some very useful tips that will help you in your relationships with others, personal and professional.

- **Work together**. Two people working together can accomplish far more in a period of time and do it better than two people working separately. This is one of the most important reasons to create and enhance great relationships personally and professionally. This concept works for a couple in a marriage raising children or a captain and copilot working together to fly a complex airliner across the Atlantic Ocean. This applies to just about any other situation imaginable in life.
- **In the professional world, be responsible *to* others, not *for* them**. Whether it is your business partner, customers, employees, or employer, you have a responsibility to these individuals to perform your work to the best of your ability. There are lines that should never be crossed, though, such as working overtime without pay in order to "save" a company that is near bankruptcy because of poor management decisions. They are not going to save you from your poor decisions, and you should never do that for them. You are not responsible for insulating others from the consequences of their behavior. When people do that, they are actually shorting themselves and setting a precedent for others to do the same.
- **Prioritize people who are interested in you over those who are interested in what you have or what you do for them**. Impersonal relationships

like the employee-employer relationship can be a necessary part of life and are to be valued, but keep in mind that they are a means to an end, not the end. Performance-based relationships are there to support our personal ones that are far more important—our relationships with our spouse, children, siblings, and so forth. Performance-based relationships are temporary and impersonal. Enjoy these relationships as much as you can, but for these reasons, keep them in perspective. Even one close personal friend has a more positive effect on your happiness and satisfaction in life than a thousand coworkers at some big corporation.

- **Keep company with the right people**. If you keep company with people who are responsible with their money, you will tend to become like them. If you spend your time with people who spend extravagantly to impress people and are reckless financially, their ways can rub off on you. Carefully pick your friends. Even the best people can be negatively influenced without even realizing it.

- **Never compare yourself or your financial situation to others based on their outward appearance.** It is both impossible and unwise to quickly judge the true financial success of other people by outward appearance. I have personally known people who, with their fancy homes, expensive cars, and flashy clothes, looked like they were rich, but later I found out that behind the scenes, their lives were both a financial and relational mess. Conversely, I knew a humble-looking, gray-haired older gentleman who drove around in an old looking Ford pickup truck. He used to pull up to the airport hangar where I worked and would get into his $1.5 million turboprop airplane and fly to Cape Cod for long weekend getaways. I personally know that this man really did have the money and knew how to manage it well. But I did not learn that overnight.

- **Save the best of yourself for those you really know, and never give your best first**. A perfect example of how to apply this can be seen when a business first hires an employee. When someone is hired initially with just about any company, he or she is hired under a probationary period during which the employer can end the employment for any reason. Sometimes employers actually have a "weeding out" period in which they are harder on new employees than they are on established ones for the purpose of determining character and trustworthiness. Higher pay, promotions, and sometimes benefits are withheld until the employee proves to be competent and someone that the company is interested in keeping for the long term. The company is being good to the employee right away by providing a job, but the best is saved for a later time after it is wise for the company to do so. You can apply this idea to every new person—personal or professional—who comes into your life. Of course, you want to be good to everyone, but it is wise to save the best for the people that you know well. Doing this will act as a safety valve that will prevent you from giving too much to someone that you don't really know yet. When it comes to new relationships, take it slow and get to know people before any serious involvement of any kind. To keep more of your money, be good to everyone that you can, but save the best for later.

One of the most effective ways to keep more of your money is to clearly differentiate between your personal relationships and your performance-based relationships. The most valuable, satisfying relationships are good personal ones. These people are interested in us and we in them. These are the people that comfort us when we are down and help us in time of need without expecting anything in return. We should be willing to do the same for them. Unfortunately, there are countless millions all over the world who have prioritized their career over their spouse and, as a result, get divorced and end up with less money than they started with! The sad reality is that most people that do this do it for people who, in most cases, do not really care about them personally. Why put yourself through all that? Sometimes keeping more of your money in the long run means making less in the short run. Getting that big promotion or raise at work means nothing if it means that you are going to lose half of what you own in five years because of a divorce caused by job stress—not to mention the toll it may take on any children you might have.

Now let's talk about the whole reason that you are reading this book: money. It is important to understand that money is a tool to serve us and other people. When you understand that, your life will work much better.

Consider a famous individual for a moment: Elvis Presley was a lonely, unhappy shell of a man when he died, from many accounts. He had riches and fame, but his personal life and relationships were a mess. I use this example to illustrate that money all by itself will not make you happy, especially if you have no good relationships in your life. Money is a tool that serves us and our families. A tool is only as good as the person using it. Some people, as a result of overindulgence and a lack of self-control, have actually destroyed their lives with money. To avoid this, you must love and respect people (including yourself) and use money—not the other way around. When you do this, your money will be much easier to manage because it is in its proper place. Your goal is to shrewdly manage money so that it serves you and your relationships, both personal and professional.

Let's move on and talk about material things for a moment. Like money, things exist to serve us. We are the boss! Problems come when we serve things and things control us. Consider the guy who makes $40,000 a year and drives a new $70,000 sports car. Unless he has some other means of income, he is more than likely working a ridiculous amount of hours a week to make large monthly payments—not to mention that he is probably feeling a great deal of stress knowing that he owes so much. He is spending money that he doesn't have to impress people whom he doesn't know and who don't really care. You are smarter than this guy. Every material thing in your life should serve you—if you are serving it, then get rid of it! Only own what you can own stress-free. It is better to drive a '99 Honda Civic with peace of mind than a new BMW with a home full of fighting and tension. It is important to place peace over possessions—always. Later on, when you can peaceably afford the BMW, go for it and enjoy yourself.

Consider, also, the personal computer. You can use it in a way that puts more money in your pocket, or you can use it in a way that wastes money. It's up to you. You can use it to do research and learn how to fix your leaking kitchen sink by yourself and keep hundreds of dollars in your pocket that you would otherwise have spent to pay a plumber. Or you can use it to gamble on the Internet and waste your hard-earned money. Recently, I have encountered people who, despite working in dead-end jobs, habitually waste their valuable time playing video games together online instead of using the *same* Internet to find better jobs. The computer is a great resource for keeping your money and making more when used properly. When you use material things (including money) wisely, you will be asking those things, "What have *you* done for *me* today?"

Now we are going to discuss the people whom you should avoid having in your life at all costs. These people will not only hurt your finances but may also hurt you if you let them get too close. Do yourself a huge favor and steer clear of these personalities if you can.

- **People who always have a need to prove themselves**. These people will bend steel and break teeth to do something, even if there is no real reason to do it. This behavior stems from a deep sense of insecurity and the need to constantly prove their own worth. You want to stay away from these people because many of them spend money constantly to impress others. The problem is that while they are making themselves look richer, they are in reality becoming poorer and more indebted. These types of people might keep a business open even though it is obviously not going to make it, just to protect their fragile ego. Even people like this who actually have success and money will never be satisfied, because no amount of outer success will fill their inner need for approval. If you work for people like this, you are on a never-ending treadmill, because most of the time they will expect you to work extra hard to support their image. It will not end until you end your relationship with them.

- **Authority-resistant people**. These people think that laws and regulations are only for people who are inferior to them. They view the rules as childish and unnecessary, because they know better than everyone else. These people can get you into trouble with authority and cost you more than money just by association.
- **Impulsive people**. These are people who simply cannot resist urges to spend money. Because of their impulsive nature, they do things and make decisions based on knee-jerk reactions and raw emotions rather than rational thinking. They make no attempt to resist the negative tendencies of human nature. These people will spend themselves into the ground and take you with them if you are close enough.

- **Helpless people**. These people simply refuse to take any responsibility for themselves or their situation. Sometimes they even demand that others provide for them because of their perceived helplessness. Even when they have opportunities to improve their lives or their finances, they don't bother trying. I am not talking about people who are sick or incapacitated in any way, or the very young or very old. I am talking about otherwise capable people who *choose* to be helpless.
- **"It won't happen to me" people**. These people think that they are invulnerable to the negative things that can happen when one is not careful in the perilous world we live in. They believe that somehow they are not susceptible to pitfalls like everyone else and that only other people do dumb things that get them into trouble. They are naive and refuse to believe the reality that you can work a lifetime for your wealth and it can be gone in five minutes if you are not careful.
- **"One way" people**. These are extraordinarily selfish people who think that the whole world revolves around them. As long as you are in a relationship with them, you will always be giving more than you will ever get back. This will not only drain your wallet but will waste time that you could be investing into healthier relationships that benefit both of you at the same time.

Great people are, and always will be, the greatest asset you will ever have in life. As stated earlier, people who are in good relationships share burdens, work together to solve problems, and help each other when they are down. They also enjoy the good times together. Families are actually the most economically profitable institution ever known to man. Think of all the necessary systems that can be present in the traditional family—the simplest forms of government, healthcare, education, social security, and even a correctional system. Is it possible that focusing on obtaining the benefits of these systems at the smaller family level is more economically feasible than spending an exorbitant amount of money trying to attain them at a much larger government level? Just look at what has happened here in America. In the last fifty years, we have seen the cost of government increase to a staggering level while the family unit has decayed to its worst state ever! You can decide if my theory is correct.

Let's end this chapter with a real-life story about a person who kept a lot of his money just because of great relationships with other people. This story is about a man I'll call Harry. Harry was a cooking instructor at a vocational school here in the United States where he started working in the 1960s. During his time there, he and many of the other instructors became very close friends. They would go camping and have picnics together. Everyone in the group would help each other outside of work anytime one of them had a big project to undertake. Because every one of his instructor friends taught a different vocation, together they had a broad amount of knowledge and experience that they used to help one another. Their friendship not only made their work time more enjoyable and satisfying but also benefitted them outside of work as well. When Harry built a new home for his growing family in the early 1970s, his friends all pitched in and helped him in every way imaginable. They all helped him move his family's things from the old house to the new with their pickup trucks. The TV repair instructor put up the TV antenna. The plumbing instructor hooked up their washer and dryer. The carpentry instructor put up all of the curtain rods for them. The drafting instructor found a mistake in the house's design prints in which the washer and dryer closet dimensions were actually too small to fit the appliances that Harry and his wife had. He even redesigned the closet so that they would fit. He also showed Harry's wife how to make paper cutouts of all of their furniture to lay onto the house's blueprint in order to help organize the move. The horticulture instructor designed the layout of the landscaping and even had some acquaintances of his come and assist in making the design a reality. Harry saved a ton of money, time, and aggravation thanks to his friends who helped him. Everyone in the group would help the others and everyone reciprocated, including Harry. Over the years, Harry cooked at his friends' wedding receptions, made wedding cakes, and helped to build a patio, put up a fence, pour sidewalks, and even build a garage, to name only a few things. This group of friends would also go to each other for advice about their home, car, or anything else related to any one of the vocations taught by their fellow instructors, saving all of them time and thousands and thousands of dollars over the years.

To enjoy life at its best and to keep more of your money, choose the right relationships.

2. Be a Big-Picture Person

As we discussed earlier, no one else in your life has as much power to act in your own best interest as you do. Because of this fact, you are in effect the manager or CEO of your own life and its decisions, like it or not. Not that we control everything and everybody, but by managing our actions and reactions wisely, it gives us a measure of control over our lives and our finances. You need to be the CEO of your own life decisions, because if you don't, someone else will. Even the most decent and honest people will almost always stack the deck in their favor, not yours. It's just human nature. Keeping more of your money requires that you take charge of your life and act in your own best interest as much as you can in order to counterbalance others doing the same. If you don't, you'll lose!

In the last twenty-five years, I have worked in all different kinds of businesses, and you must know one of the skills that managers in any business must possess: the ability to see the "big picture," assess it accurately, and act accordingly to both prevent and solve problems. The big picture is the entire perspective on a situation or an issue. Big-picture thinking takes into account all of the factors involved in a situation, what is happening now, and what will happen next. Good managers use all of this information wisely to maximize profit and minimize losses. The best managers are so perceptive that they see potential problems so far ahead of time and act so early and accurately that no one even knows that a problem would have occurred. Even if you never want to be a manager in a business, you can learn from these people and apply the lessons to your personal situation to give yourself an advantage.

Now let's look at some examples of a good manager and a bad manager.

Imagine that it is Saturday night. You decide to go to your favorite restaurant with a friend on the spur of the moment. When you get there, there is a line of people out the door and down the side of the building. You want this problem fixed so that you can get in and eat, right? In order for this to happen, the management has to fix the problem.

The good manager looks at the entire restaurant and figures out that people are not getting seated fast enough because the tables are not being cleared fast enough. The good manager then takes a prep cook who is preparing tomorrow's food (which is bound to be a slower day at the restaurant), has him change uniforms quickly, and now he is a bus person! The tables are cleared faster, the line moves quickly, and you are in and sitting in little time. After you order, your food comes quickly. You eat and enjoy yourself. As you leave, there is still no line.

Now imagine that a couple of months go by and you decide to go to the same restaurant. You arrive and see a line again. You're not worried, however, because this happened the last time you showed up, but you got seated quickly and had a good time. Unfortunately, though, the situation is a little different this time. The bad manager is on duty.

The bad manager sees the same problem as the good manager did: the tables are not being cleared fast enough. His actions are different, though. He starts clearing the tables himself and quickly loses sight of the "big picture." Now the line starts moving and you are seated quickly, but you place your order and have waited forty minutes and still don't have your food. This happened because while the bad manger was clearing tables, the grill in the kitchen malfunctioned and slowed down the cooks. The manager did not know this for some time because he was distracted with clearing tables, and it took the kitchen staff a while to find him in this very large restaurant with many rooms. He gets back to the kitchen to fix the grill, but it takes another fifteen minutes before the grill is working again. Because of this, you have to wait over an hour to get your food. By the time your food comes, you are so disgusted from waiting that you don't enjoy your food. You may never eat there again, and many customers feel the same way. This restaurant may lose thousands in future business, all because one person failed to see the big picture and take the proper steps to fix a problem.

In order to keep more of your money, you must become the manager of your own life, relationships, money, and career. No one on planet earth can or will do a better job than you will—not financial advisors, the government, your boss, or anyone else. Because you are your own manager, everything starts with the big picture. Of course most of us cannot always delegate details to someone else, but our actions and reactions should all focus on the big picture first; details come second. When you do this, details (like money) are easier to manage. Big-picture thinking tends to put you more in the planning business, rather than the reacting business.

Here is another example of applying big-picture thinking. A couple in their late fifties decides to buy a piece of land and build the home of their dreams—a huge two-story house with many rooms. After really thinking about it, they reconsider and decide that it should just remain a dream. Their reasons are many. First of all, since in general most people become less physically able to take care of a home as they get older, it would be unwise to start this project at this stage in their lives. Second, they have seen that even a modest home like the one they have owned for the last thirty years can go through stages that require lots of expensive maintenance, especially after it is about twenty years old. They do not want to be going through this stage while in their seventies and on a fixed retirement income. In addition, they do not want to burden their children with having to help around their house all the time, because their children all have homes and families of their own now. And if they do have to go into a nursing home at some point, they will only have to move one more time. Their wise decision will probably save them tens of thousands of dollars, as well as countless hours of work and possible aggravation not just for them but also for their children and grandchildren.

There are so many examples of very educated, intelligent people doing things that hurt them financially because of inattention to the big picture. A very successful businessman that I know sent his very intelligent son to college to get an engineering degree here in the United States. He was unable to find work in his career field after graduation. I saw him a year or so later, and he still was not working as an engineer. If they had just looked at the big picture, they would have seen the hard reality that there have been fewer and fewer jobs here for engineers in the manufacturing industry since the 1980s. Why would anyone really be surprised that this happened? This happened because of ignorance of the big picture. Even the most intelligent people can make this mistake. It is very sad to not do what you love as a career, but it is even worse to pay the price anyway. I met another young man who graduated from one of the best aviation colleges in the United States with a commercial pilot's license and a bachelor's degree in aviation science—all to the tune of $200,000 dollars. His intention was to become an airline pilot. According to him, this college promised him that it had all the connections for job placement that he needed upon graduation, but he got nothing in writing when he enrolled. Two years after graduation, this college still could do nothing for him as far as finding him work as a pilot. When I met him, he was working part time as a flight instructor in a tiny flight school making about as much as a dishwasher makes. If this poor guy had just looked at the hard reality of the aviation industry here, he would have seen that in the big picture, the airline pilot profession has been going downhill since the late 1970s and got drastically worse after the events of September 11, 2001. Now this young man will be working hard to pay off the debt and the interest for decades. This poor decision will probably affect every aspect of his life for the rest of his life, including his future marriage, children, and possibly even his children's education. I present these examples not to make fun of these two young men but to impress on you the immense importance of big-picture thinking in *your* life to help you make the right decisions *now*.

Here are some of the best and most important big-picture truths to help you keep more of your money.

- **The world today is not fair or nice**. As a matter of fact, it is a battlefield. Anyone who thinks otherwise is naive. Try to go out into the business world with a positive but sober attitude. Remember that your power in life lies in your actions *and* your reactions to what happens out there. You cannot control everything or everyone, nor should you seek to, but you must recognize that to be your own best friend, you need to act *and* react in the best way possible to what happens in order to benefit you and those around you the most.

- **The old-fashioned work ethic no longer works**. If you work hard enough, you will eventually be successful—this old-fashioned work ethic used to work years ago here in the United States because the majority of people were decent, moral, and ethical. But it doesn't work anymore. There are still many people like this, but there is a large percentage of people here today that are immoral, selfish, and dishonest, and the number of them is growing. Hard work is worth nothing to you if it is put into the wrong place. The new work ethic is that work is necessary for success in anything, but your hard work should only go into *the right places* where you *and* the other party are both winning. You should be constantly evaluating where your hard work is going. Sometimes companies change ownership and become different places that are no longer worthy of your efforts. Other times it is because technology has changed your career field. No matter the reason, be careful where you work because it is very possible (and very easy) to fall into situations where you are working hard and going nowhere.

- **If you let someone control your mind, he or she can control every aspect of your life**. One of the best ways someone can steal from you is by getting you to believe something that is not true. Many people right now are working like dogs for large companies because they believe that it will get them somewhere in life when, in fact, it will not. What is really happening is that the imagined "success" that these people are slaving and competing for is actually just a mirage put in front of them in order to get them to work hard to make someone else very rich at their expense. This kind of deception is commonplace at many places of employment today. If you work for a company like this, leave, because you are never going to win there. Many people here in the United States believed that their 401(k) retirement accounts were bulletproof and would grow forever no matter what happened. History tells us how false that belief was. Another belief that is prevalent today in the United States is that you *must* have a college education to be successful. Really? Then why do such a high percentage of millionaires in the United States have no college education? Go to college if you need to for your career choice. But in all areas of your life, be careful of what you believe to be true. Do you have any erroneous beliefs that are allowing others to steal from you *right now*?

- **Order attracts, maintains, and multiplies wealth**. When things are organized, wealth is attracted to it. When you shop at a department store, you like to spend your money in a nice, clean, neat, well-lit store where you can find what you want, right? The worker whose desk is clean and neat and has his projects done on time and in the way that the boss asks for them tends to attract promotions and raises. Creating and maintaining order in every area of your life—your marriage, your business, and even your car's maintenance— is key to keeping your money and making more in the future.

- **Disorder tends to repel wealth and cause financial loss**. Let's imagine that you go to get your car fixed at a certain garage and the mechanic accidentally leaves a wrench on top of your engine after he is done working on your car. He closes the hood; you pay your bill and drive happily down the road assuming that the repair was properly and thoroughly done. Suddenly, you hear a loud noise coming from under the hood. It sounds like your car engine is coming apart, because the wrench that was accidentally left behind fell into the spinning belts and pullies on the front of the engine and is now destroying the belt and the engine accessories. Your car is now undriveable and must be towed back to the garage to be fixed. Now the garage must pay for the tow bill to get your car back to the garage. They have to suspend work on another customer's car because they have to pull a mechanic off of it to come and tow yours, making the other customer angry and jeopardizing future business with that customer. And that is before they have to pay to fix your car properly. To top it all off, they will probably lose your future business—all because a wrench was left where it didn't belong.

- **Everything progresses in cycles, and everything is always changing**. Life is a cycle. We are born as babies, we grow up, some of us reproduce, and then unfortunately we die. We don't live forever, and we don't make money forever. If you are making lots of money right now, invest wisely and plan ahead for the time when you are not making money. If you are broke, keep trying to better your situation, because everything is subject to change—even bad things. There are people today who are not only broke but deeply in debt and homeless because they assumed that their pay, their retirement account, and the value of their home would just continue to rise in value forever. If you have a very lucrative period in your life, ride the train as long as you can but plan as if it were going to end tomorrow. When you do this, you are putting a safety valve on your success.

- **How a person handles money is very revealing about his or her character**. Did you know that when any major airline is considering a pilot candidate, one of the things that they scrutinize is the candidate's credit rating? If someone cannot be trusted to pay his or her bills once a month, why should the airline trust that person to leave the ground with a multi-million-dollar airliner, over one hundred passengers, and baggage? You can apply this simple concept in evaluating the people you might be doing serious business with. If someone is not trustworthy, he or she is not worth your time.

- **The oldest and most effective way to sell anything is to create a problem (imagined or real) and then create the solution so that someone either wants or needs to buy it**. One of the best ways to keep more of your money is to use this tactic in reverse—spend your valuable time thinking of innovative and free ways to eliminate the needs that others will use to vacuum the money out of your pockets. If you spend too much, an employer may use that to your detriment. I just met a man who used to own his own business and made a lot of money running it. What he told me was this: "When I looked for employees, I always wanted to hire a man who has a big house, an expensive car, and a wife that has expensive taste so that he has to **work hard**." Why? Because the individuals with an expensive lifestyle needed to work hard so that they could maintain that lifestyle, which would ultimately make money for *him* and *his business*. Yes—it is true: spending too much creates needs that some people can and will use to *their* advantage if you let them. The people who have the most freedom in this world are the ones who do not need anything! They get the privilege of only having the people in their lives whom they choose. What needs can you eliminate in *your* life to keep more of your money?

- **The natural flow of the world is negative**. Unfortunately, many of us are surrounded by people and situations that are negative. But we can refuse to let this force us into negative patterns. One common negative is that many people work very hard and wind up with very little to show for it. So why do some of us spend so much time imitating these people? To keep more of your money, forget what everyone else is doing and do what is best for *you*! Keeping more of your money means being willing to be different when necessary, even if it costs you the approval of others. If you want different results than most people, then you must do things differently than most people. Here is a simple example. When an economy in a certain country is booming, most people are out spending money. There is a much smaller group of people who, during this same time, are saving and investing. When the economy dumps out, they have money because they did the opposite of what most people did. This smaller group of people is then usually called by two different names: wealthy or rich!

- **As long as there are human needs and desires, there is always money to be made**. What changes is where it is being made. While one industry fails, another is growing. I just heard a man talking about how he made more money during the 2008 recession than he has ever made in his entire life. He is a multimillionaire. Why are we surprised when a manufacturing plant closes, the stock market crashes, or houses stop selling? This has happened before, and it will happen again until the world ends. Let's plan for it and think of ways to actually profit from it instead of reacting to it. That is what some of the richest among us have done to become rich.

- **Hard work should be a means to an end, not the end**. In any endeavor, from starting a business to beginning a career, we will have to work very hard in the beginning, but it should become easier over time until we are getting increasing reward for our efforts. If what you are doing is not getting easier or serving your purposes after an appropriate amount of time, it is time to reevaluate what you are doing. Some of the wealthiest people in the world worked very hard in the beginning, but because they got increasing reward for their efforts, their lives are much easier now. If they still work hard, it is because they want to, not because they have to. Remember to enjoy yourself on the way to the end, too. Many people delay today's gratification and enjoyment of people and things for some magic land "out there" in the future—somewhere that they might not ever see in reality. Working and planning for the future is great, but enjoy yourself on the way there, because tomorrow is not guaranteed for anyone. Enjoy the journey to the intended destination, and you will get the most out of your time here.

- **Gold and silver are the only true forms of money**. For thousands of years, these two precious metals have been used to store value and to transfer wealth. They have remained to this day both valuable and recognizable, and they always will be. The problem is that most of the "money" that is used today is not actually money but fiat currency that has no backing or connection to anything of real value like gold or silver. The first problem with this is that every unbacked currency always eventually becomes worth its intrinsic value, or zero. The other problem with this is that any currency unconnected to real valuables is subject to tampering and manipulation by the issuing authority, such as printing and digitizing worthless paper and electronic currency to pay expenses and debts. Why then, you may ask, does the price of gold and silver go up and down? The answer is simple. The intrinsic value in the gold and silver is constant, and the currency price reveals how valuable the currency is—not the metal. The main reason gold is so expensive today is because the currency has become worth much less. The best way to store wealth and value today is with real tangibles that can be seen and touched, as long as you have a way of safeguarding them.

- **Technology has changed the world and continues to change the world**. The world has changed more in the last one hundred years than in the previous thousands of years. Technology has sped up life and the rate that things change to a ridiculous pace. One of the problems with this is that it makes career selection very difficult for younger people today. It is possible to choose a career, go to college for four years, and by the time you graduate, the career field you chose has completely changed or evaporated altogether! This is a serious problem, considering the cost of a college education today. If you are considering going to college or technical school, do yourself a huge favor and take the time to really find out if the career field you are choosing will still be there for a while. And make sure to get independent advice from someone who does not have anything to gain or lose from your decision. Never blindly trust the college or trade school staff to make your choice. The best advice comes from people who are business owners or employees *currently* working in your prospective career field.

- **Technology can open you up to many problems**. Someone on the other side of the world can make a computer virus that crashes and destroys your computer, costing you hundreds and possibly thousands of dollars. It is okay to use technology like computers, cell phones, and so forth, but do not wholly depend on them for your survival. Be good to yourself and be prepared for technology failure at any time. Our technology infrastructure is made by humans and is subject to fail and break down, just like anything else man-made. In order to work, it depends on thousands of people whom you don't know and have no control over.

- **The main difference between the monetary classes is how they spend their money**. This is a simple concept that is rarely taught. What you do with your money once it gets in your hands is where the power of decision is. Of course, this does not guarantee what class you are in, but here are the general spending habits of each class: The wealthy buy things that make money for them first, like businesses, investments, intellectual property, and real estate. The middle class buys things that cost them money every month, like houses and cars. The poor buy stuff that is instantly worth almost nothing as soon as they buy it. What monetary class do you want to be in?

- **The casino concept is not just at the casino**. If you have ever been to a casino, you know that these places are visually impressive and extravagant, and some can be immense, with some of the most unbelievably wild architecture anywhere. They are meant to "wow" you and make you *feel* rich and important just by being there. The reality of these places is about as depressing as they are impressive to look at. First of all, this glamour is all built to lure you in to *lose*. No one spends millions to build a casino to lose money. The house always has the advantage. There is really nothing there for you to gain, because only a tiny percentage of people walk out with more than they came in with. Most lose. The money you spend there is not an investment but a loss, actually creating more need for you to earn more money. You experience a few passing moments of fun, and then it is back to reality. Why is this information important even if you never go to a casino? The reason is because other places that you *do* go to use the same techniques to suck the money out of your pockets. Shopping malls, large electronic stores, and fancy restaurants and clothing stores all can use the same tactics! They can lure you in with their fancy appearance for their profit. It is almost impossible to name one thing that you can buy at one of these places that is actually an investment. You may actually need some of the things there, but most of what you buy is worth a tiny fraction of what you just spent the second you walk out the door with it. The house won again! We all enjoy these places, and it is good to do so periodically as an *occasional* treat, but just remember that the money and time that you spend there is just that—spent! As long as you remember that they are there for someone else's profit and not yours, it becomes very unappealing to frequent these places too much. In the area where I live, there are thousands of stores like this that are everywhere and easy to find. But there are only three or four places to actually buy investments, and most of them are hard to find because they are in tiny, unimpressive locations like in a small building or strip mall. I would bet money that it's the same where you live. To keep more of your money, remember the casino concept.

- **Most systems of the world are set up by others, for others, and work against the common person**. Unless you are one of the privileged few, there are two sets of rules—one for you and another for those in power. The government, the money system, the tax system, the stock market, and even the system of pay at many places of employment are against the common person from a financial standpoint. They are composed of people whom you don't know, and the rules are made to give them the advantage. For the most part, it has been this way since the days of the Pharaohs in Egypt. There is one small group with most of the power, money, and influence calling all the shots, and then there are the rest of the people in the country or organization that are just used as a means to their ends. Yes, there are some exceptions of good governments and companies that are actually for the people, but even here in the United States where the government was originally intended to be by the people and for the people, that is no longer the case. To keep more of your money, stop looking to these systems to get ahead. To counteract them, make it a top priority to act in *your* best interest and value quality personal and professional relationships above all others. This is where *your* prosperity is. Be honest and follow the rules, but work to get things that you need outside of these systems as much as possible. Some of you reading this book are hardworking, honest, and diligent but aren't getting anywhere because you are trying to win in a system that was designed to work against you as an individual, such as in a country with an oppressive government or in a company with a corrupt pay system.

Now let's talk about how being a big-picture person can help you in your everyday life. Big-picture thinking helps you to get to the root of financial problems as quickly as possible. Let's suppose that you are in a dead-end job that is not only miserable to be at fifty hours a week, but that is making your whole life miserable. It is straining your relationship with your spouse and your children, not to mention taking a toll on your bank account. This situation must be fixed quickly because this employer who does not give a hoot about you will run you into the ground if you let him. Let's imagine that you have one week of vacation to use this year. You will not gain much if you only escape from your miserable existence for one short week and then have to go back for another fifty-one. So what you are going to do is sacrifice your week of temporary escape and use it to go out and look for a permanent solution that improves your whole life by using it to job hunt or to take steps to fix the real problem, which is your relationship with this employer. Even if you do not find a better job, at least you can sleep at night knowing that you did everything you could to improve your life. Sadly, many people work jobs they hate just for the money and then have to spend thousands, if not tens of thousands, to go on extravagant vacations to "escape" and blow off the steam that built up from their unhappy lives. If you love your work, you won't feel like you have to get away as much, and part of your pay is enjoyment and contentment, which, by the way, is not taxed!

To keep more of your money, BE A BIG-PICTURE PERSON.

3. Be Careful of the Little Things

All of us want to be more financially secure and have more money in the years ahead, right? In the last chapter, we discussed how to do this by focusing on the big picture first. In this chapter, we will discuss the little things in detail. This chapter and the last one may seem to contradict each other, but actually, they must be applied at the same time. As we will learn in a later chapter, all of the "things" in your life can be made to work together not just to save you money but to make your whole life easier.

It is difficult to save money or give oneself more disposable income by cutting back on larger expenses like mortgage, rent, and transportation. So what can be done to accomplish this? Determine which little expenses will turn into large ones over a long period of time. This is so effective because it is easier and much more painless to adjust small expenses than large ones. Today it seems like there are more small things to buy than ever before—all kinds of gadgets and gizmos, most of which we do not need and that wind up in the dump a few short years later. We also live in the age of five-dollar nutrition bars, gourmet coffees, and energy drinks. These seemingly small items bought regularly and frequently will blow a huge hole in your monthly budget for how little they do for you. Here are some other relatively unimportant things we can spend money on that will break our budgets if bought too frequently: magazines, meals at restaurants, and even cheap cups of coffee at convenience stores.

While we are on the subject of convenience stores, if you frequent them, it must be said that visiting these shops less often will be one of the single most effective ways to put more money in your pocket. What is so convenient about them, anyway? You can go to a regular grocery store once a week and get everything you need as inexpensively as you can, or you can go to a convenience store several times a week and pay up to five times as much for some items. If your job's schedule or location requires you to frequent them, it is a large hidden cost of doing business for your employer, unless they pay for this. If you own a convenience store, don't worry—not everyone will read this book.

Let's talk for a moment about the $1.69 cup of coffee that some of you buy at the convenience store every morning on your way to work. In ten years, even if you figure in two weeks of vacation a year when you probably wouldn't buy it, that cup of coffee will cost you $4,225! But wait—that money you spent was after income taxes, right? If your tax rate is 20 percent, you had to actually earn $5,281 to pay for one cup of coffee a day for ten years! How much could you have if you had invested this money? Do you have many of these little things that you buy every day draining your wallet? You can see how damaging that little cup of coffee is to your long-term savings or investment. As a rule, if you have money to waste, you have money to invest.

Here's a real-life example of how damaging it is to have expensive little habits that waste your money over time. This story is about me. It is embarrassing, but I must share it because it demonstrates how stupid it is to waste what is perceived to be just a small amount of money over a long period of time. I picked up the habit of smoking when I was about thirteen. My dad smoked, and I always thought it to be glamorous and pleasurable. I was dumb enough to try it—and I liked it. As I got older and had more freedom and easier access to cigarettes, I smoked more. By the time I was sixteen, I was smoking a pack a day. In all, I smoked for about twenty years. I recently took a calculator and estimated that I spent about $25,000 on cigarettes during that twenty-year period. Today, I have nothing to show for all that hard-earned money that I wasted on cigarettes. Now just imagine that instead I invested that money and made it into $35,000. I can think of a lot of things that I could do with that money right now! What a waste. Please use my story as a warning to not do this yourself or as an incentive to stop if you are doing something similar. The sooner you stop, the sooner you'll keep more of your money. As I said, **if you have money to waste, you have money to invest!**

Now let's talk about another category of "little things." These are seemingly small or insignificant things that can create sudden large expenses, financial disaster, or in some cases even death if engaged in recklessly or not maintained properly.

Several years ago, I heard a true story about a man who, because of one of those little things, could have lost not only everything he owned but also his life. This man had satellite television. That winter, there was a really bad ice storm, and as a result, this man's satellite TV dish on his roof became covered with ice, knocking out his signal. He went up on the slippery roof to clear off the ice and—

you guessed it—he fell off. From what I remember, he broke his back in many places, as well as his pelvis. The doctors were not sure that he would ever walk again, and he had a family to support.

I do not know what happened to this man later, but I can only hope that today he is fully recovered. I use this story not to make fun of him (haven't we all done dumb things?) but to learn from him. If this man had stopped for thirty seconds to think about the "big picture," or what he had to gain versus what he had to lose, he probably would not have tried this. Even a week later, the inconvenience of not having TV for a day or so would have been long forgotten. But now, his grandchildren will probably be telling the tale of grandpa falling off the roof after the ice storm. This event may have affected his family for the rest of their lives—all for a little thing like no TV for a brief period of time.

It can be equally detrimental to your finances to not pay attention to little things that should be properly maintained. Here is an example. On some cars and small SUVs, there is a part in the engine called the timing belt. This belt, to put it simply, synchronizes all the internal engine parts so that the engine will run. As long as it is replaced at certain intervals, like every sixty thousand miles, it will almost never fail or cause a problem. On some vehicles, however, if this belt is neglected and snaps, some of the internal engine parts will actually collide, causing catastrophic failure of the engine. This can make a perfectly running engine junk in a matter of seconds! The timing belt itself usually costs less than $100, and if you pay a repair shop to change it, your bill will usually be less than $400. If it breaks, however, it can cost you thousands to replace the engine. Some older vehicles that would have otherwise provided additional years of reliable service can actually be totaled because the cost of an engine replacement exceeds the vehicles' value. All of this can happen because of not properly maintaining a belt that costs less than $100! There are so many little things that can "get you" if you are not careful. Even something as simple as staying home when using your washing machine can save you hundreds, if not thousands: if you are home and able to take care of an overflowing washing machine right away, you will save a good deal of money not fixing water damage had you otherwise not been home to mop up the mess immediately.

To keep more of your money, be careful of the little things, because in the end, they are just as important as the big things.

4. Do It Right the First Time, and Finish What You Start

A wonderful truth that will keep more money in your pocket and work for you in anything from buying a home to getting married to planning a career is this: in all undertakings in life, from the small to the great, you will get the most out of your money, time, and effort when you do it right the first time and finish completely with as little interruption as possible. Of course, none of us are perfect, and no one does everything perfectly the first time. Nevertheless, this should be your goal in everything you do, because when you can get away with it, you get the most profit from the least amount of output. This is a good goal to have, right? But don't worry—the whole next chapter is dedicated to what you can do when you don't do things right the first time.

One of the best ways to do anything without a hitch is to first make sure that what you want to do is wise! Intelligence and knowledge are highly esteemed, but wisdom is above them both. Think of it this way: wisdom dictates why you should or shouldn't do something, while knowledge and intelligence tell you how to do something.

So what happens when you don't do something right the first time? Let's start with one of the simplest examples I can think of—buying socks. Suppose you go and buy yourself a package of socks. You knew the socks were low quality, but you bought them anyway so that you could save a few dollars. Several weeks later, they are full of holes. Now you have to go and buy socks again. If you purchase a poor-quality item just because it's cheaper in price, it's likely that that item will not last long and you will, as a result, have to buy it again, which will end up costing you more than if you would have just bought the better-quality, but more expensive, item in the first place. Now imagine this effect being repeated dozens of times a year as a result of the multitude of cheap items some people buy today. This makes it easy to understand why some people and some families who make good money wind up broke or, at best, really have nothing to show for what they make.

Now let's talk about an example that has a lot more at stake. Let's imagine that you work for a good company that wants to promote you with the condition that you have to move to another state within three months. You accept the offer. Because you are under pressure to find a home, you buy one hastily. You start working at your job, and a few months go by. There is a lot of rain one week, and as a result, you find out that the house's foundation leaks, because the basement is flooded. You now have a repair bill for the foundation that will cost you over $10,000. Consequently, you have to spend all of the extra money you make your first year there on the foundation repair. If you had had time to have someone look at the home more carefully, this may not have happened. Stories like this happen in real life every day.

Going back to the example of the socks, let's now imagine that you spent a few extra bucks to buy the better socks. Because you bought the good socks the first time, you are now able to "finish" the business of keeping good socks in your drawer because good socks will last a long time. Remember from chapter 1 that material things exist to serve us. When we do things right the first time—whether it's buying a package of socks, getting married, buying a car or house, or planning a career—we get the most out of everything for the least amount of money, time, and effort.

One of the simplest things that you can do to get things done right the first time is to simply slow down. In our fast-paced technological world, there is constant pressure on us to do more and to make it happen faster. Do you notice that we have cell phones and computers that do things with lightning speed but somehow we are getting shortchanged because we really don't have any more free time than we did in the past and no one is really any happier? We are doing more than ever before, but are we doing those things well? Is "progress" making us go forward in some ways but backward in others? There are multitudes of people who allow themselves to be pressured into doing things hastily only to have to do them again. Some of the hastily made mistakes have consequences that can't be undone. Be good to yourself and simply refuse to do anything at a time or pace that isn't good for you. The longer you give yourself to think about anything before doing it, the better the result generally. If you do not have peace of mind about doing something, don't do it!

To keep more of your money, do it right the first time, and finish what you start.

5. Turn Negatives into Positives and Make Mistakes Work for You

In the previous chapter, we discussed that in order to get the most from your money, your goal should be to try to do things right the first time. This chapter is dedicated to what you can do about mistakes—not just yours, but those of others as well.

Mistakes are an inevitable part of our human existence. Even the most brilliant and accomplished people make them. Of course, you want to make as few as possible. But because it is impossible for you to avoid them altogether, you can actually manage them to help you keep more of your money! You can even use mistakes that are not yours.

We can learn something about this from the major airlines of the world. Even the most lucrative and financially healthy airline knows that one accident can cause not just an immense financial loss of millions of dollars but also, and more importantly, the tragic loss of human life. Because of the safety-sensitive nature of aviation, airlines have to be very picky when deciding whom to hire as pilots. There are no perfect people and, therefore, no such thing as perfect pilots to hire. So how do airlines decide which ones to choose? Well, one of the first and most critical parts of the process is to divide the applicants into two groups. One group will be able to continue on in the selection process, and the other will be shown the door and never invited back. The group that is allowed to continue in the selection process is the group of imperfect applicants who have learned from their mistakes and are unlikely to repeat them. The other group that is shown the door and are never asked back are the imperfect applicants who have demonstrated that they do not learn from their mistakes and may possibly repeat them in the future. You can keep more of your money by applying the principle that the airlines use. In your personal life, you must be very careful about who you do any serious business with. One of the best ways to avoid unnecessary troubles that will cost you money, time, and frustration is to absolutely refuse to do serious business with those who don't learn from mistakes. That means prospective or current employees, employers, or business partners. You may even apply this to choosing a prospective marriage partner if you are not yet married.

Keeping more of your money, or succeeding at any other pursuit imaginable, is critically dependent on what you do, or don't do, about your mistakes. There is no crime in making a mistake—the crime is only committed when you fail to learn from it. Every time you use the experience of a past mistake to prevent a loss in the present, you are in effect making that mistake pay you back.

Yes—it is true that our mistakes can actually benefit us in the long term! But it costs us something to learn the lesson. Unfortunately, the world can be a harsh and unforgiving classroom, and some of the mistakes cause consequences that can affect the rest of our lives. But what about the mistakes and pitfalls that others make? They are a source of wisdom that we can get completely free and without consequences to us. That free wisdom and understanding will help you keep more of your money.

Here is a true story that serves as a perfect example. In 1995, a man I'll call James bought a house. He had a home inspection done but decided to skip an optional test of the well's water pressure that would have cost less than $200. This test determines whether a well is likely to go dry. James bought the home since, to him, the water pressure seemed okay. Unfortunately, however, there was minimal rain the following summer, and his well went dry. As a result, he had to take out a loan for $5,000 to pay someone to drill a new well. That inexpensive well test probably would have pointed to a problem, which would have meant that the bill for drilling the new well would have been paid by the previous owners before he bought the house.

James has a friend named Bill. While buying his first house in 2004, Bill remembered the hard lesson James learned, so he decided that even though it was going to cost almost $800, he was going to get a thorough home inspection done. He even decided to get all of the optional tests done that were not required for the bank to approve his loan—two of which were a well water test and a septic system test. The well water test found bacteria in the water. This problem required the installation of a UV water filter, which the previous owners had to pay for, to the tune of almost $1,000. The septic system test found a problem that cost thousands to fix. Bill kept thousands of dollars in his pocket by learning from someone else's mistake.

To keep more of your money, turn negatives into positives and make mistakes work for you.

6. Put a Limit on What You Lose

Even the most successful financial investors have bought investments that either didn't grow or actually lost value. What do they do when this happens? The smartest investors always try to put a limit on how much money they are willing lose. For instance, online investors who use Schwab.com can place what is called a stop order on any stocks that they own. What this can do is tell Schwab.com to automatically sell a stock when the price per share falls to a certain price in an attempt to limit what the investor loses on the stocks. Even if you never want to be an investor, you can apply this simple concept of loss limitation to your personal life to keep more of your money.

To apply this principle of loss limitation, first identify those things in your life that are the most valuable to you and that are worth protecting. They can be things like your health, your spouse, your children, or your home. Obviously, the more personal and irreplaceable something is to you, the more it is to be guarded, and the more you are probably willing to give to keep it.

Second, you need to understand that everyone else is just as important as you are, and you want to try to treat everyone in your life the way that you would want to be treated. You still need to have less-personal relationships in your life like coworkers, business associates, employers, and so forth, but problems with these lesser relationships can affect the more important ones if you are not careful. Again, these people are just as important as you are and you should treat them as such. But since people of less personal importance *to you* are limited in what they can do for you, you must limit what you are willing to lose for them. This is a simple common-sense concept.

In life, people will fail us. Even things will fail us, like cars. But when that happens, you can be smart and limit the effects in the interest of protecting everybody and everything else. To keep more of your money, you can limit what you lose by keeping your eye on what is really important to you and protect it by refusing to let the less significant affect it.

Here's an example of a practical application.

Let's suppose you have a good job that provides a good living for you and your family, but there is a coworker that keeps starting arguments with you. Even though he is wrong, this person is putting you in the potentially dangerous position of losing your job if you keep arguing, because your employer could just get tired of the whole thing and get rid of both of you to end the problem (which makes the important point that it is indeed possible to win an argument and end up actually losing much more). I could write a whole book on how to handle disagreements with coworkers, but since we don't have time for that, I will just boil it down for you here. To limit the cost of these arguments, you don't try to win them. You instead calmly approach the management and explain the situation. From then on, you don't argue—no matter what. You must keep in mind that allowing this person to bait you into another argument could cost you your job, your family's financial security, and many other things that are valuable to you. Limit what you lose for this person who, in the big picture, means little to you. Refuse to argue, and let the other person get himself fired if he refuses to stop. In the end, you and your family win.

A practical way to limit what you lose is to avoid situations that create these sorts of questions: How long will you work that dead—end, go—nowhere job? How long will you keep that business open that is losing money? How much money will you spend to keep up with what the family across the street has? How much money will you put into that lemon of a car you bought that costs you hundreds in towing and repair bills every time it breaks down? How many times will you bail out that friend who keeps getting thrown in jail for driving under the influence? When you continue doing things like this, you are putting yourself in a situation where you are no longer in control of how much time or money you are going to spend. To keep more of your money, never allow yourself to get into situations where other people or their actions are dictating what you spend. Help others only as much as you can without hurting yourself. Remember— you are responsible *to* other people, not *for* them, unless it is a close personal relationship.

Another way to limit what you lose is to limit what you spend on certain products that you buy. For instance, if you want to keep more of your money, simply avoid buying newly released models of cell phones, computers, cars, TVs, and so forth. I know this is not for everyone; some of you reading this book love to have the latest and greatest the minute it comes out, and I respect that. If that is you, you'll probably want to skip to the next chapter.

The rest of this chapter is for those who are willing to wait. Just because you wait doesn't mean that you can't ever have these products, but by simply changing the timing of when you buy them, you save not only money but oftentimes a lot of aggravation, too.

Let's talk about why it is good to wait. All of these items are good to have, and most of us enjoy them. Items like cell phones can actually enhance your personal relationships, but it is important to understand that unless you are using these items to make money, they are not financial investments (the best thing about a cell phone is not the phone but the person on the other end if he or she is someone you like). Yes, you may enjoy these products for a while, but from a strictly financial perspective, they depreciate very quickly, and after a certain period of time, they are all eventually worth nothing. These items actually turn your hard-earned cash into air. You can go to a yard sale today and find items that were hot even two years ago being sold for a fraction of the price paid originally. Also, you need to understand that even as you are buying that new cell phone or computer, the replacement is already planned that will make what you are buying right now obsolete. It is planned that way to put you on a never-ending treadmill that is purposely designed to make others wealthy. Remember—these things are good to have, but it is not good to pay a lot of money for them for these reasons.

It is astronomically expensive to produce new versions of technology products like cell phones and computers. Manufacturers spend many years and millions of dollars to develop these products. Understandably then, when the new items first go on sale, the companies that produced them want a return on their investment. In order to do this, they have to charge not just for the materials and labor expended to make them, but for the research and development as well. Also, when the latest and greatest of any product comes out, that is usually when the demand is highest, adding even more to the price.

To limit what you lose when buying these items, wait until the price comes down. Let other people pay top dollar for those items that will become instantly worth less the minute those people walk out the door of the store they bought the items in. How much less you spend when you eventually do buy those items depends on how long you wait. Remember—no matter how long you wait, they will always be new to *you* when you eventually buy them. You may even appreciate them more because of the wait. The more you wait, the less you spend. If that new-model UHD TV cost $1,500 when it first came out a year ago and you buy it today for $900, you spent $600 less. You kept more money for yourself by doing nothing but waiting. This is a great way to work smarter instead of harder and get the same result with much less work.

Another reason to wait to buy newly released items is that these items usually have the most problems when they are first released. This is an ugly truth that company advertisement will never tell you. Most people think that when a new item like a new-model cell phone is released, all the product testing is finished. The reality is this: the final test of a new product is when it gets into the hands of the consumer. Real-world consumer use is actually the most difficult and thorough testing for any new product design to pass. When you buy a newly released product, not only are you paying top dollar for no reason, but you are actually volunteering to be a product tester without being on that company's payroll.

While new items may come with a warranty, two things that you will not be compensated for if problems arise are wasted time and aggravation. To keep more of your money and your precious time, let someone else pay top dollar for these items and test them for you; then you can buy them for less and enjoy them with fewer problems.

To keep more of your money and to take care of the important people and possessions in your life, put a limit on what you lose.

7. Make All Things Work Together for You

To keep more of your money, you can manage all of the different things in your life—your relationships (personal and professional), your career, your talents and skills, your home, and even your personal possessions, when you are able—in an orchestrated and organized manner that benefits you. You also must manage the positive and negative circumstances that will come your way. The goal is to use everything that comes your way, positive and negative, to work for you. Your actions and reactions to life's circumstances are the only things over which you have any real power, since you can't control everything. It is also important to understand that we live in a world where one can do everything right and still wind up with nothing to show for it. If you are one of these people, then I can identify with you. It has happened to me many times. If this is the case for you, keep doing your best because many who are persistent win in the end simply because they refuse to quit.

In order to manage all of the different things in your life in an orchestrated and organized manner that benefits you, there are three principles that you have to understand first.

1. As stated earlier, your own health, peace of mind, and personal relationships are the most valuable things you have. Everything else is secondary.

2. There are countless things that have value besides money. How much do you value your legs when you see someone who doesn't have any? How much money would you have to make to compensate for not being able to take care of that aging parent whom you love so dearly during the last years of his or her life? How much did money mean to someone trapped in the Twin Towers on September 11? You get the idea.

3. Not everything in life is good, but negatives can create positives. For example, most businesses in the world exist to provide solutions to problems—where would broom companies be if there were no dirty floors? In fact, life can be overflowing with negatives at times. In a world that has more than enough selfish, careless people who only care about Number One, negative events are just a natural occurrence. The people who are going to make the most money in the years ahead are the people who create solutions to the many serious problems that are present in the world today. These people will actually make the negatives work for them. Take LifeLock, an identity-theft protection company, for example. Identity theft is a huge global problem that has ruined many lives. LifeLock is a stable, profitable company because it offers people a solution to a horrible problem. And the worse identity theft gets the more money LifeLock will probably make. Conversely,

positives can create negatives, like when a successful, lucrative company gets sued because of a jealous competitor, for example. Obviously, we don't seek the negative, but if it comes, we try to use it to our advantage.

Anyone can profit from positives. To keep more of your money, you can manage the positive *and* the negative together to work for you. Look for ways to do this in every situation that comes your way.

Here is an example of how I did this. During a period in my life, every career path I had tried to go down didn't work out. I did everything I could to make them work but got no results. Finally, I ended up working for a construction company, which was my last choice for a career. Quite honestly, I hate construction and did not enjoy it one bit. But since I needed to pay the bills to keep my home, I stayed there for eleven years. During my time there, I was suddenly exposed to a business in which I had almost no experience except for the very basic carpentry skills I learned from my dad, and a couple of years of wood shop in high school. Before I knew it, I was asked to do things like build walls, install doors and windows, and repair roofs, which I had never done before. I ended up using these new skills that I had unintentionally acquired to do jobs on my own house, saving me thousands on home repairs. I tore down the rotten outer half of my screened-in porch deck and completely rebuilt it with new wood. I even built brand-new stairs and handrails that were better than the originals. I removed and replaced the siding on both sides and two corners of my garage. I did dozens of little roof repairs and was able to maintain it myself using my newly acquired skills. I refurbished one of my closets and put in new drywall and shelves. My kitchen badly needed new windows during that time, and since I was able to buy windows at cost through the company I worked for, I jumped at the opportunity. The man who did most of this company's residential window installations helped me put them in for free since he had become a friend. The list goes on and on. I was not happy about working in the construction field, but I took advantage of my circumstances and as a result, saved thousands of dollars. These new skills keep more money in my pocket even today and probably will for the rest of my life.

Here is another thing that I took advantage of while I was working there. Because one of my many duties was to drive a construction material delivery truck, there was a lot of boring time on the highway. I had a lot of time to think about my life in the last twenty years and ponder all of the things that I had done right and wrong. I also thought about my successes and failures and those of other people I know. That is where many of the concepts in this book came to my mind.

Here in America, many view money, position, and power as things of paramount importance. Many people think that the high-paying corporate position is one of the best things you can have in life. Yes, there are indeed a lot of positives that can go with this if you are one of the few who actually achieves this position and stays there.

Let's talk about some of the perks that come with these positions. You may have a huge paycheck that most only dream about. You may have prestige and the privilege of a private corner office, four weeks of paid vacation a year, and even the use of the company airplane, if it has one. Yes, there can be many positive things that work for you. But that isn't really the whole story.

The truth is that while there are many things working for you if you have this high-paying position, there also can be just as many, if not more, negatives simultaneously working against you that may negate all of the positives in the end.

First of all, here is something to think about. When you start working for any large corporation, most of the time you will be placed in a system of unintentional relationships. You will be working for, with, and around a large group of people whom you don't really know. Since the employees and management are just a cross section of society in general, you will have good people and bad ones. This simple fact alone can cause problems that you may not even know about even after investing years of your life into the company—problems that can affect you, your family, and your money, even if you do everything right.

Another thing that you need to understand is that you are investing in something that you do not own. To get to such a prestigious corporate position, you would have probably had to work very, very hard—more than likely at the expense of your family. Long hours, the stress and responsibility, and time away from home can result in the loss of certain things that you can't put a price on, like seeing your children grow up—all to earn a job that could be here today and gone tomorrow.

In no way am I trying to tell you what to do or not do with your life. The purpose here is to lay all of the chips—good and bad—on the table to help you in your decisions.

You can see from the example that, yes, there can be many good things to gain from that high-paying corporate job, but the negatives might, in some cases, outweigh the positives. Many people have said that they sacrificed their marriage, their relationship with their children, and even their health to climb to the top of the corporate ladder—only to find an empty, lonely, and impersonal existence there.

Now we will look at a real person who, by outward appearances, was very successful but who actually had a lot of problems working against him as a result of his "success." Luke was a pilot who had a very lucrative job flying for a freight airline. He made almost $100,000 a year as a captain of a large cargo aircraft. He worked a very easy Monday-through-Friday schedule, and he only flew a few hours a day, spending the rest of his day relaxing between flights. He had a wife and a son of about ten whom he sent to a private school.

Luke spent many years working low-paying flying jobs in order to get the experience for his current job. While he was working as a flight instructor, he went broke, partly because of the very low pay, but also because he had to pay child support for a son from a previous marriage. It was years before he had any money again. After flight instruction, he got a slightly better-paying job flying night freight in a single-engine airplane. At this point, he was finally able to start unburying himself financially, but this job put a strain on his marriage and was a hindrance to quality family time. And up to this time, he still had not been able to invest much money or save for retirement, while many people his age had been doing so for years.

Finally, after years of sacrifice that had taken a toll on his marriage and his finances, he landed a good job as a first officer with a well-paying freight airline. He finally made enough to really support his family well and had opportunity for advancement to captain. But since this company was an on-demand air freight business, he was on call 24/7, which continued to strain his family relationship and made it almost impossible to plan family time or social events. He also had to go and receive recurrent training classes several states away, where he would be gone for weeks at a time. This caused lapses in communication between him and his wife that strained their relationship even more.

Then an unexpected change happened to the company that he worked for. In 2008, the automotive industry here in the United States was hit hard by the recession. The auto industry was one of his company's biggest customers, and this fact allowed him to be based near his home in North Carolina and spend his off time with his family. But now, he had to accept an assignment based out of Texas flying a contract freight route for an international freight company. His schedule required him to be in Texas for six weeks at a time and at home for two. At this point, although he was making almost $100,000 dollars a year as a captain, he now had to establish and pay for another residence and an additional vehicle in Texas. During his off time while he was away, he was not doing anything really constructive and was unable to spend any time with his family except on the phone. Sometimes he had to go out and spend money he would not normally spend just because he was bored in his little apartment. At the same time, the regular maintenance on his primary residence that he could have done himself was not being done. His son missed seeing him and would probably have been a much happier boy if he had seen his dad more.

When Luke finally did get home for his two weeks off, he spent most of it catching up on household maintenance, mowing, and cleaning that he was unable to do when he was away, which ate up his valuable family time. His wife did a great job of taking care of things while Luke was gone, but she just couldn't do it all herself. Some of the household repairs he could have inexpensively done himself he now had to pay someone else much more money to do simply because he didn't have time to do them. He made a lot of money at his job, but it cost him a lot to have it—not just monetarily but in other ways that you can't put a price tag on.

Luke was a successful professional pilot, but his success created many unintended consequences and circumstances that constantly worked against him. A couple of years ago, he really started to realize that the root cause of his problems at the time was his career choice. He loved to fly airplanes for a living but was seeking employment in other capacities in the aviation field and work closer to home so he could eliminate these problems. In his own words, "Everything has to work together." Obviously because of his employment at the time, this was not the case. Even though he did what he loved for a living and it was a success, he did not really understand when he got started in his career all of the negatives that came with this profession. What happened to Luke had nothing to do with bad luck. Luke actually saw many problems with his profession early on, but instead of limiting his losses and changing careers early, he continued to press on until he paid a huge price that no amount of money could compensate for. The best way for you to count the cost of a potential career that you are considering is to seek those who are currently employed in the field, ask them what the negatives are that they have to deal with, and soberly consider whether or not to go that route *before* you spend time and money to get there.

A positive example is Joseph-Armand Bombardier, born in 1907 in Valcourt, Quebec, a rural Canadian town. He was gifted with amazing ingenuity, inventiveness, and mechanical skill. Even as a boy, his talent became obvious. He built an operating miniature locomotive powered by a clock mechanism. He took an old broken gun and created a miniature cannon from it that actually fired. He even made a working steam engine from old sewing machine parts. A concern of Joseph's during his youth was the limited ability of people to travel during the winter. At the age of fifteen, he built a "snow machine" that was basically a four-runner sled with an engine, an airplane-style propeller on the rear, and a simple steering system. His father was pleased with his son's achievement, but he made Joseph dismantle it because he thought it was dangerous.

As a young adult, Joseph studied mechanics and electrical engineering, and served an apprenticeship in a garage. He eventually opened his own garage in 1926 and continued working on and designing new snow machines with limited practical utility or commercial success.

In 1929 he married and started a family. Five years later, in the winter of 1934, Joseph's two-year-old son, Yvon, became ill with an inflammatory condition of the abdomen lining called peritonitis. Sadly, Yvon died from this condition because his family was unable to get him proper medical attention due to their rural isolation and the harsh winter environment. Joseph and his wife were devastated. But Joseph refused to let the grief of this loss debilitate him. Instead, he was more determined than ever to make his snow machines a solution for the dangers of rural winter isolation in Canada.

In 1935, he developed a new drive system for his snow machines that would be instrumental in the success of later versions. He continued working tirelessly on these machines for years, even while people mocked him and made fun of his inventions. By 1937, his snow machines looked like cars with a fully enclosed cab, a track on each side in the rear, and two skis for steering in the front. Many improvements continued to be made. By the time the post–World War II years had arrived, his snow machines were used as ambulances, rescue vehicles, school busses, and even postal service vehicles. In the late 1950s, Joseph developed the prototype for a smaller, lighter version of his snow machine that was for personal use. Production began and his new personal snow machines were branded "Ski-Doo," the name still used today. This basic design is the parent of the modern snowmobile and is used by all snowmobile manufacturers today.

Since its creation, Joseph's invention, the snowmobile, has saved thousands of lives all over the world. Through the years, the company he began has employed thousands of people. Today, two companies are descendants of his original company, L'Auto-Neige Bombardier Limitée. One is Bombardier Recreational Products Inc., which manufactures snowmobiles, ATVs, personal watercraft, and small jet boats. The other is Bombardier Inc., a multinational company employing people around the globe that designs and manufactures trains and jet aircraft for commercial and business use.

Joseph-Armand Bombardier died in 1964 a wealthy businessman and successful entrepreneur. He lived a short but very full, productive, and fruitful life. Joseph made *all* of the things in his life—the good *and* the bad—work together for him and those around him, leaving behind an invention that has saved countless lives and a legacy of human achievement and progress.

Consider asking yourself these questions: What things in my life can I use to keep more money in my pocket? What good things could be causing unintended negatives, and are they really worth the price that I am paying for them? What negative things can I use to my advantage, or to make more money?

One final point that will help you make the most out of the information presented in this book is this: Applying any one of the principles in this book, especially those found in chapter 1, will help you keep more of your money. But when you use *all* of the principles in this book *together*, you will get the most benefit possible.

To keep more of your money and to have a more fulfilling life, make all things—the negative and the positive—work together for you.

Conclusion: Is Everything in This Book Really True?

Should you believe the principles I've shared in this book? Consider the following: "Billy Joel has gone bankrupt three times and lost about $90,000,000 thanks to some help from his ex-brother-in-law who managed his money."[1] I think it's safe to conclude a number of things from this statement:

- **Making money means nothing unless you know how to keep it**—this is obvious here.
- **It's important to choose the right relationships**. Billy had the wrong person managing his money.
- **Looking at the big picture**, there must have been a huge problem if a musician making millions kept going broke.
- I think it is safe to say that all of the money was lost **a little at a time**, since no one would purposely try to waste all of that money at once.
- When it comes to money management, they did not **do it right the first time** and did not **learn from their mistakes, either**.

---

[1] XFINITY music programmers, "Billy Joel," *No Money, Mo' Problems* (slideshow), accessed August 4, 2012, view content at www.KeepMoreMoneyBook.com/BillyJoel/.

- No one was making any effort here to **limit any losses**.
- Billy made his musical talent work for him to make him millions of dollars. Unfortunately, he did not make **all** of the things that he had control over **work for him** to ensure that he kept more of his money.

The evidence speaks for itself, doesn't it?

Legal Disclaimer

Keep More of Your Money is for the purpose of information and entertainment only. You use this information at your own risk. Michael Andrews and Sarel Information Products, LLC, have no liability for any outcomes or consequential damages from the use of the information in this book. All investments mentioned in *Keep More of Your Money* are for the purpose of example only. Michael Andrews is not an investment or financial advisor and does not recommend investments or financial strategies to anyone. For investment, financial, legal, or tax advice, please consult with professionals that are legally certified in these areas. Any corporate entities mentioned or references to trademarks are for the purpose of example only, and there is no association.